1948

MILESTONES, MEMORIES,
TRIVIA AND FACTS, NEWS EVENTS,
PROMINENT PERSONALITIES &
SPORTS HIGHLIGHTS OF THE YEAR

TO :

FROM :

MESSAGE :

*selected and researched
by
betsy dexter*

WARNER TREASURES™

PUBLISHED BY WARNER BOOKS

A TIME WARNER COMPANY

COPYRIGHT ©1995 BY
WARNER BOOKS, INC.
All Rights Reserved.

Warner Books, Inc.
1271 Avenue of the Americas
New York, New York 10020

Warner Treasures is a
trademark of Warner Books, Inc.

A Time Warner Company

DESIGN:
CAROL BOKUNIEWICZ DESIGN
PRINTED IN SINGAPORE
FIRST PRINTING : SEPTEMBER 1995
10 9 8 7 6 5 4 3 2 1
ISBN : 0-446-91082-1

This was the year spy mania gripped America. **Whittaker Chambers**, himself a confessed ex-spy, accused former top state department official Alger Hiss of giving him secret government papers and being a member of the Communist Party. Chambers told the House Un-American Activities Committee of a "Red underground" operating in federal posts.

The Selective Service Act authorized the registration of all men 18 to 25 and drafting of men to create an army of 837,000, a navy and marine corps of 666,882, and an air force of 502,000.

In New York, the largest airport in the world, Idlewild International, was dedicated.

General Motors signed the first sliding wage scale union contract with the United Automobile Workers. It included a clause that adjusted wages to the cost-of-living index.

President Truman ordered an end to discrimination in the Armed Forces.

newsreel

THE UNITED STATES RECOGNIZED THE INDEPENDENT JEWISH STATE OF ISRAEL.

In one of the major upsets in American history, **Harry S Truman** was reelected president over Republican favorite Thomas E. Dewey. Southern Democrats, upset with Truman's stance on the race issue, bolted the party to nominate Governor Strom Thurmond on the States' Rights Ticket.

On January 12, in a unanimous decision, the Supreme Court ordered the state of Oklahoma to admit a Black student, Ada Lois Sipuel, to the University of Oklahoma Law School.

The Soviet blockade of all rail and road traffic between Berlin and the West led to a large-scale airlift by Western powers to West Berlin.

Daniel François Malan, an advocate of apartheid, became premier of South Africa.

The Organization of American States was established to work with the UN to promote peace, economic growth, and national sovereignty.

In **Czechoslovakia**, Communists staged a coup, toppling the government and taking complete control. By the end of the year Communists had gained full control of Hungary.

headlines
international

On January 30, Mahatma Gandhi was shot and killed by a fanatic Hindu Nationalist in New Delhi, India.

As the British mandate over Palestine ended, the Jewish state of Israel was proclaimed with David Ben-Gurion as prime minister and Chaim Weizmann as president.

Arab armies from Lebanon, Syria, Jordan, and Egypt attacked Israel.

North Korea proclaimed its independence as the People's Democratic Republic of Korea.

An international tribunal in Tokyo sentenced former Japanese Prime Minister Hideki Tojo to death by hanging.

The state of Kansas repealed Prohibition after 68 years.

The Smithsonian accepted the original Wright Brothers plane, *Kitty Hawk*.

The U.S. Air Force began Project Blue Book to investigate flying saucer reports.

Harry Truman campaigned the old-fashioned way this year, passing up the modern convenience of an airplane for the traditional campaign train. His whistle-stop tour kicked off in June. Supporters shouted "Give 'em hell, Harry!" from coast to coast.

With 45 billion units of penicillin and hundreds of radio ads, New York attacked 250,000 "hidden" cases of venereal disease.

The Supreme Court ruled that religious instruction in public schools was unconstitutional.

In October, the House Un-American Activities Committee implicated Charlie Chaplin.

cultural milestones

Indiana professor **Alfred Kinsey** shocked America with his book *Sexual Behavior in the Human Male*. He asked 5,300 white males about the frequency of masturbation, orgasm, oral sex, petting, and marital and extramarital intercourse.

Georges Braque won the Grand Prize at the Venice Art Festival.

radio

NEWSPAPER EDITORS OF AMERICA TOP RADIO STARS OF 1948

Champion of Champions **Jack Benny, Fred Allen, Bing Crosby, Arthur Godfrey**

Comedian **Jack Benny, Fred Allen, Bob Hope**

Comedienne **Eve Arden, Gracie Allen, Judy Canova**

Comedy Team **Fibber McGee and Molly, Amos 'n' Andy**

Mystery Show **"Sam Spade," "Suspense," "Inner Sanctum"**

Quiz Show **"You Bet Your Life," "Twenty Questions," "Who Said That?"**

Two future TV stars kicked off radio sitcoms this year. In "My Favorite Husband," Lucille Ball played a wacky wife whose escapades made life hell on her banker hubby, Richard Denning. "Our Miss Brooks" featured Eve Arden as Connie Brooks, a wry but levelheaded teacher at Madison High.

television

On February 16, "Camel Newsreel Theatre" became NBC's first nightly news show.

In the fall, NBC changed the name of its "Puppet Playhouse" and gave birth to TV's first superstar—Howdy Doody. "The Howdy Doody Show" was a major hit out of the gate. Buffalo Bob Smith was the genial host, as well as the voice of popular regulars Phineas T. Bluster, Captain Scuttlebutt, and Howdy, himself. Bob Keeshan—later Captain Kangaroo—played the mute clown Clarabell.

science

Yale University scientists developed a nylon respirator to replace the dreaded iron lung.

Eric Jacobsen, a Danish pharmacologist, introduced the drug disulfiram for treatment of alcoholism. A patient taking the drug and using alcohol would become violently ill.

Physicist **Richard Feynman** developed an improved theory of quantum physics.

Oak Ridge National Laboratory began to develop peaceful uses for atomic energy.

celeb divorce

Orson Welles and Rita Hayworth were divorced this December, which did not stop them from appearing together in *The Lady from Shanghai*, which Welles wrote and directed.

celeb births

MIKHAIL BARYSHNIKOV, dancer and actor, January 28, in Riga, Latvia

ALICE COOPER, rock star, in Detroit, on February 4.

BARBARA HERSHEY, actress, in Los Angeles, on February 5.

JAMES TAYLOR, singer-songwriter, in Boston, on March 12.

DIANNE WIEST, stage and screen actress, Kansas City, MO, on March 28.

RHEA PERLMAN, "Cheers" star, wife of Danny DeVito, on March 31, in Brooklyn.

STEVIE NICKS, Fleetwood Mac member, in Phoenix, on May 26.

RICHARD SIMMONS, hyper exercise guru, July 12, in New Orleans.

RUBEN BLADES, singer, activist, and actor, in Panama City, on July 16.

KATHLEEN BATTLE, opera star, Portsmouth, OH, on August 13.

NELL CARTER, actress, Birmingham, AL, on September 13.

JEREMY IRONS, actor, Cowes, England, on September 19.

PRINCE CHARLES, randy royal heir, in London, on November 14.

GERARD DEPARDIEU, actor, in Chateauroux, France, on December 27.

DONNA SUMMER, disco queen, in Boston, on December 31.

DEATHS

Orville Wright, American aviation pioneer and brother of Wilbur, died on January 30.

Sergei Eisenstein, Russian filmmaker, director of masterpieces *Ten Days That Shook the World* and *Ivan the Terrible*, died in the USSR on February 10.

Antonin Artaud, French actor-director and radical poet, died on March 4.

Wilhelm von Opel, German auto pioneer and Nazi auto manufacturer, died on May 2.

Claude McKay, the Black American Marxist poet, died at 58, on May 22.

Louis Lumiere, Pioneering French photographer, died on June 6.

Charles Evans Hughes, 11th chief justice of the Supreme Court, died on August 27.

Babe Ruth, 53, died on August 16. The Sultan of Swat hit a record 60 home runs in the 1927 season and 714 homers overall.

Charles Beard, distinguished American historian, died on September 1.

milestones

'48 hit music

MILLION SELLING RECORDS

nature boy
(Capitol), Nat King Cole with an orchestra conducted by Frank de Vol

just a little lovin' will go a long way
(Victor), Eddy Arnold

because
(Victor), Perry Como with the Russ Case Orchestra

the fat man
(Imperial), Fats Domino

Fats Domino's smash hit "The Fat Man" represented the 1st New Orleans rhythm-and-blues million-seller. The novelty hit of the year was Don Gardner's nonsensical little-kid song "All I Want for Christmas Is My Two Front Teeth," as performed by Spike Jones.

BALLROOM DANCING

The El Comrnando, or mambo rumba, was the ballroom dance craze of 1948. As tourists flocked to South America, the samba soared in popularity. It was far easier for stiff-limbed Americans to master than the rumba.

Top Male Radio Vocalists
Bing Crosby, Perry Como, Gordon McRae

Top Female Radio Vocalists
Dinah Shore, Peggy Lee, Jo Stafford

Top Classical Male Vocalists
James Melton, Robert Merrill, Ezio Pinza

Top Classical Female Vocalists
Rise Stevens, Marian Anderson, Lily Pons

Top Dance Bands
Vaughn Monroe, Guy Lombardo, Tex Beneke

fiction

1. **the big fisherman**
   by lloyd c. douglas
2. **the naked and the dead**
   by norman mailer
3. **the bishop's mantle**
   by agnes sligh turnbull
4. **tomorrow will be better**
   by betty smith
5. **the golden hawk**
   by frank yerby
6. **raintree county**
   by ross f. lockridge, jr.
7. **shannon's way**
   by a. j. cronin
8. **pilgrim's inn**
   by elizabeth goudge
9. **the young lions**
   by irwin shaw

Dale Carnegie and positive thinker **Norman Vincent Peale** weighed in this year with two books in the self-help category, catering to a war-weary America that just wanted to feel good about itself. **Evelyn Waugh** aimed his satirical eye on California, penning *The Loved One*, about a Los Angeles mortician. South African novelist **Alan Paton** published *Cry, the Beloved Country*, about racial strife-torn South Africa.

books

nonfiction

1. **crusade in europe**
   by dwight d. eisenhower
2. **how to stop worrying and start living**
   by dale carnegie
3. **peace of mind**
   by j. l. liebman
4. **sexual behavior in the human male**
   by a. c. kinsey
5. **wine, women and words**
   by billy rose
6. **the life and times of the shmoo**
   by al capp
7. **the gathering storm**
   by winston churchill
8. **roosevelt and hopkins**
   by robert e. sherwood
9. **a guide to confident living**
   by norman vincent peale

In baseball, **Satchel Paige**, a pitching legend in the Negro Leagues, was signed by the Cleveland Indians. The veteran hurler claimed to be 39, but admitted "I might be in my fifties." He was really 42.

The Indians went on to break a tie with the White Sox to win the American League title in the first-ever playoffs. Cleveland then took the World Series, overcoming the Braves, 4–2.

At the 5th Winter Olympics, the U.S. took the gold in men's figure skating, but placed 4th overall, behind Sweden, Norway, and Switzerland.

Stan Musial of the St. Louis Cardinals won the National League's Most Valuable Player Award for the 3rd time.

In auto racing, Mauri Rose won his 2nd Indy 500 in a Blue Crown Special, racing around the track at a breakneck average of 119.8 mph.

In tennis, Jack Kramer beat Bobby Riggs to take the 21st pro tennis title at Forest Hills.

sports

In horse racing, Eddie Arcaro rode Citation to victory in the Kentucky Derby, the Belmont, and the Preakness, to win the vaunted Triple Crown. Arcaro was the first jockey to win the Derby 4 times.

In college football, Yale elected Levi Jackson captain, the first time a Black man had held the position in the Ivy League.

At the **Summer Olympics** in London, the U.S. snagged 38 medals, making an unprecedented sweep of the swimming events. The highlight of the Games was the victory of 17-year-old Robert Mathias, a native of Tulare, CA, in the grueling decathlon.

ARMY AND NAVY TIED, 21–21, IN THEIR ANNUAL GRIDIRON MATCH.

oscar winners

Best Picture **Hamlet,** Rank/Two Cities, produced by Laurence Olivier

Best Actor **Laurence Olivier,** Hamlet

Best Actress **Jane Wyman,** Johnny Belinda

Best Supporting Actor **Walter Huston,** The Treasure of the Sierra Madre

Best Supporting Actress **Claire Trevor,** Key Largo

Best Director **John Huston,** The Treasure of the Sierra Madre

Best Original Screenplay **The Search,** by Richard Schweizer and David Wechsler

Best Adapted Screenplay **The Treasure of the Sierra Madre,** by John Huston

hit movies

1. *The Red Shoes* Rank-Archers/Eagle-Lion ($5,000,000)
2. *Red River* United Artists ($4,506,825)
3. *The Paleface* Paramount ($4,500,000)
4. *The Three Musketeers* MGM ($4,306,876)
5. *Johnny Belinda* Warner Bros. ($4,266,000)

TOP 10 BOX-OFFICE STARS
1. Bing Crosby
2. Betty Grable
3. Abbott and Costello
4. Gary Cooper
5. Bob Hope
6. Humphrey Bogart
7. Clark Gable
8. Cary Grant
9. Spencer Tracy
10. Ingrid Bergman

movies

Humphrey Bogart teamed with director John Huston this year in the classics *The Treasure of the Sierra Madre* and *Key Largo*. Ballet soared in popularity in England after the war, and *The Red Shoes* reflected this popularity. The film was expected to flop horribly in the U.S., but surprised everyone. The highlight of the film was the 20-minute performance, in the middle of the story, of the ballet *The Red Shoes*.

KEY LARGO

More than 1,000 dual-control cars were loaned by the auto industry for high school drivers' education programs.

Willys-Overland introduced a 6-cylinder Jeep station wagon and a convertible called the Jeepster.

Goodrich introduced tubeless tires.

cars

The 100 millionth car was produced in the United States

The 1948 Cadillac featured tail fins inspired by Lockheed's P-38 fighter aircraft. This luxury ride sported a 2-piece curved windshield and extra wide rear window.

Pleated skirts were fashionable everywhere—pressed, unpressed, box, inverted, sun-ray, accordion and knife—worn over taffeta petticoats in bright colors. Spring evening gowns with panniers—an extension of Dior's New Look fullness—were featured. Bodices were generally tight, with deep décolletés. An asymmetrical line was emphasized, particularly on evening gowns, which had one-shoulder-and-one-sleeve bodices and wrapped-and-draped torsos.

SHOPPING SPREE

Man's virgin wool suit **$58**
Man's hat **$8.50**
All-wool worsted ski sweater **$9.95**
Wool flannel dress **$17.98**
Young man's overcoat **$55**
Man's athletic shorts **$1.45**
Child's snowsuit **$13.95**
Pigskin belt **$2**

fashion

Tweed was big news this year.

A light, almost silky texture was now available in America in a variety of patterns and colors. Quite different from old-fashioned, traditional tweed, this fabric was considered smart enough for town suits.

Protesting the Dior Look, which featured skirts that fell to about 10" off the floor, a group of women calling themselves **The Little Below the Knee Club** marched outside the designer's hotel in Chicago.

VOGUE incorporating Vanit

Tailored by
Max Levine
NEW YORK

Muted plaid worsted in
ROBIN HOOD GREEN.
Slim lines ... beautifully
tailored in the inimitable
manner of Max Levine.
Sizes 10 to 18. Under $100.

For the name of the store in your city w
MAX LEVINE & CO., 205 W. 39th St., N

final factoid

The first woman was sworn into the United States Army.

credits

archive photos: inside front cover, pages 1, 6, 10, 15, 20, 24

associated press: pages 2, 3, 5, 7, 16

photofest: pages 8, 10, 13, 18, 19

photo research:
alice albert

coordination:
rustyn birch

design:
carol bokuniewicz design
paul ritter

'48